DOUBLE TAKE

DOUBLE TAKE

George Hardy

Harold Shaw Publishers
Wheaton, Illinois

*Scripture references are from the Revised
Standard Version. Those marked TLB are from The Living Bible.*

*Copyright © 1979 by
Harold Shaw Publishers*

*All rights reserved. No part of this book may be
reproduced in any manner without written permission
from Harold Shaw Publishers, Box 567, Wheaton, Illinois 60187.*

Cartoons drawn by Annette Breukelman

Library of Congress Catalog Card Number 79-65375

ISBN 0-87788-182-0

Contents

Introduction

"Life! I never asked for it in the first place . . . but since it has already happened, I just let it keep on happening. I've never found the alternative to be all that fascinating. It's a poor excuse for living, but this way it hurts less. The future? To hell with the future . . . let's get on with the past! It takes the speculation out of it. Am I open to suggestions? Sure, but be careful—I turn off easy. Besides, this way I don't have to believe in anything! A new outlook? Why not? This one isn't going anyplace."

Probably the most revealing thing about us is our outlook. It influences our moods, the clothes we wear, the friends we choose, the things we do, even whether we succeed or fail. But what it does best is to flagrantly meddle with our future.

For most of us our outlook just seemed to arrive at the door. Not on any particular day, but unannounced, like an overly presumptuous relative, it moved in and started to run our lives. And we let it take over without ever really considering the consequences.

A lot of outlooks around aren't turning out like they were supposed to. In fact, the average outlook is becoming downright depressing. But it really doesn't have to be that way at all. There *is* a future to be had, so bright and so real that just the thought of being a part of it is totally transforming.

If you have a future you would rather not think about, then you have nothing to lose by giving your present outlook a second look. In the process you could find yourself doing a double take right into a brand new future!

1
Whatever Became of Dear Old Bill?

It may seem ridiculous to suggest that a brighter future is only a second look away. If it does seem that way, it's only because we have generally accepted all the good options being used up and even the better of the bad ones getting fewer. Over the last few decades we have had some heavies laid on us and they have taken their toll on our resiliency, our ability to bounce back to any reasonable state of optimism. We have allowed our minds to be overwhelmed by every gloomy sage who can promote a paperback—until we believe we are on our way to disaster and well past the point of no return.

The truth of it is, we are where we are because we

have accepted some very fundamental concepts about ourselves that are completely wrong—at least this is the premise of this book. These fundamentally wrong concepts are about to become our shroud, and it will take a superhuman effort from us to recognize this and to apply the necessary correction factor in time.

Our hang-ups are killing us! They are the accumulation of mental blocks resulting from our very human inclination to favor solutions more personally acceptable than credible.

How often have you heard this conversation:

Dick: "Dear Bill, that old rascal, just died."
Jane: "H'mm. I'm really sorry he passed on. Oh well, he's at peace now."

At peace now! Who says so? And where did he "pass on" to? Granted it is a very acceptable solution for dear old Bill, but when you examine the rationale behind it, dear old Bill's whereabouts become pretty uncertain!

The writer has no intention of pressing on anyone some religious cure-all. God knows enough of those are around already! Pie in the sky religions come in many flavors—and most of us at one time or another have been burned by the religious scene where everyone stands around at the foot of the mountain and waits for the bad news.

Actually, instead of becoming reconciled to a life that just keeps on happening, an alternative is available that amazingly keeps getting put down or overlooked entirely. Surprisingly enough, the best of the good options is still open and it devastates the prevailing pessimism around us. This pessimism is solely the result of wrong answers that somehow attain the respectability of popular opinion, leaving the where-abouts of dear old Bill, and many other vital ques-tions, in a hopeless muddle—a patchwork of wishful thinking.

Not to live under a cloud of pessimism, nor to be committed to purely wishful thinking, nor to be sub-dued by the hang-ups that keep us from discovering a future worth looking forward to will require a hard look at many of our most tender and long standing opinions—but it's worth it!

2
Never Say Die!

His name was Sidney Jeans. Looking at him, you felt that in his younger days he could have been a driver for Wells Fargo. Something about him made loneliness, hardship and vast distances appear quite surmountable. You could even believe that in some magic way he had been transported from the days of the Old West into the present.

On New Year's day in the Legion home they were having a little afternoon concert for those old folks who had not been fortunate enough to be invited elsewhere. The bright winter sun beat against the drapes as though sunlight in the room was a forbidden luxury. Entering the room was as nearly a non-event as any social encounter is ever likely to be. Coming and going attracted no attention at all. Everything that met the eye was old—the people in the chairs, the pictures on the wall, the cracked, painted floor—even the air was old, as though it had been used over and over again. Looking at those dear old folks it was hard not to believe that their last option had been used up, and that all they had left were the tail ends of time. Yet in the midst of this gloom was Sidney Jeans and he was something else!

Months have passed since that afternoon at the Legion home and all the faces have long since faded from memory, except that of Sidney Jeans. Was it the twinkle that never left his eye? Or was it because he seemed to be quietly enjoying his own little secret that others in the room didn't know? Anyway, in that 80-plus-year-old man there was a light that wouldn't go out. He was in total contrast to his surroundings. Everything about that dreary scene spelled "game over, finished," and he was the only one in the room that wasn't believing it! What's your secret, Sidney Jeans?

"Now here's the plan . . ."

3

Good Luck, Dauntless Dan!
(Maybe this plan will turn out even better than your last one.)

Unworkable plans aren't all that unusual. One of the things we have most in common is a life plan that has little hope of success. What's really amazing is how far we can be led down the garden path and never become suspicious. Unwittingly we are the victims of the slickest little "con job" you can ever imagine. We do it to ourselves! It has become so much a part of the life-style we enjoy that we pretend not to see the little red light flashing when the plan starts to fall apart. About the only discernable pattern in our lives is that we appear to be an ingeniously contrived device with a built-in life cycle, programmed at some unexpected moment to "self-destruct."

We pretend to be reconciled to that moment of self-destruction. For some bewildering reason we do not project ourselves beyond it. We assume so easily there is nothing more, that the entrancing human phenomenon simply vanishes without further trace. We have no need to plan beyond because there is no beyond. Strangely enough we overlook the possibility that the human race might persist far beyond the flashing red light!

The dear old Bill's of this world just seem to let life happen and take their chances. The Sidney Jean's on the other hand appear to have a game plan that goes right on into overtime. Up to a certain point one plan looks as good as another—but then, Noah's friends also seemed to have a perfectly good game plan going for them . . . until it started to rain!

4
Positive Pam:
It Can't Happen to Me

Pam's mind is set in concrete—or it's about to be! Actually Pam is involved in what is called "the slow learning process." Her mind has always been wide open to anything—except change. Poor Pam—often in doubt, but never wrong!

Dauntless Dan and Positive Pam aren't really lonely people. They have company. They have a life plan that can't work and they hold opinions that are infallibly wrong. Still, they manage to live with all the easy confidence of those who have the situation well in hand. That's faith. Or is it, once again, part of being led ever so gently down the garden path?

Ego alone can't explain a man insisting on playing out such a cold hand and intelligence by itself would have caught on long ago. But it doesn't disturb Pam to see plans very much like her own running into disaster daily. Pam is a positive thinker! She is willing to defend to the very death an opinion she picked up in the first place as casually as any bad habit. She has the same tendency to hang on to it regardless of how harmful it may turn out to be. She never seems to question its authenticity even though it has become as obsolete as the Model T. When Pam thinks she is thinking, she is only rearranging her prejudices.

But the real tragedy of Pam is that she is unwilling to see herself as part of the inevitable life cycle. She is confident she is the one exception. Very much like the butterfly impaled on the collector's pin, she keeps congratulating herself for having evaded the spider. Nevertheless you have to hand it to Pam. She's the ultimate optimist. She believes it can only happen to someone else—no matter *how often* it happens to someone else!

She is remarkably immune to a positive learning experience. Pam "learns" from her mistakes rather than from her successes. This way she becomes quite expert at what doesn't work rather than what does. She is blissfully blind to the danger that sooner or later she is bound to make a mistake that does not allow for any later correction factor. A very pleasant present is Pam's undoing. Oh well, it's only her life!

Positive Thinking

5
The Romantic Fallacy

How can one know when one is being led gently down the garden path? The very first indication is a life style that casually leaves God out of the picture. Whoops— we just lost Pam! She's shut the book. It is one of her infallible opinions that the price you pay for belief in God is your mind and your reason. Positive Pam is long gone, her mind made up, Model T and all. Her number one hang-up is God!

Most of us however will concede there is some sort of Benevolent Force to take into account, more or less. We are willing to rationalize from there. We allow that God should properly preside over our lives up to kindergarten level, but after that it is desirable to develop something a little more sophisticated for ourselves. This usually turns out to be a nice everyday platitude with intellectual embroidering—something that leaves us flexible to do as we please.

We take comfort from such signs along the garden path as:

"There is something of the divine in each one of us."

Our minds are effectively sheltered from the shock of new ideas by thick layers of cliches like:

"Nobody can really be sure."

Or that universal trapdoor:

"Just as long as you are *sincere*. . . ."

Many of us have been misled by the special fragrance of a beautiful life and its potential for good. For nostalgia's sake we exaggerate out of all proportion our hope of bringing about a better world. It helps to keep alive the romantic fallacy that the good that is in us must ultimately prevail over all that is evil.

As Robert Ardrey tells us in his book *African Genesis,* others have become reconciled to a colossal weeding of the human garden. To them, inevitably, the grand but tragic breed of man will someday pass from the earth, driven to extinction by an insatiable predator instinct. Yet for them a strange evolutionary hope persists that out of it all maybe "The Presence," "The Keeper of Kinds," will allow a few mutant beings to survive.

At one time few dared to question the inevitable upward path on which the academic disciplines had placed us. The ancient aspiration "we shall be as gods" weighed heavily upon us. But recently the Mexican artist Otaxca presented to Dartmouth College his painting which reflects some of the disillusionment now showing in this pursuit . . ."a skeleton giving birth to a skeleton, dry bones spawning more dry bones."

Yet probably the most heartbreaking scene of all was noted in *Vancouver Life* magazine. A little girl stood backstage in her black leotards, dainty and exquisite as a figurine. Dreaming out loud she recited this well-known little verse to a reporter:

> My candle burns at both ends
> It cannot last the night,
> But O my friends and O my foes,
> It sheds a lovely light.[1]

Knowingly, wistfully, she was on the garden path and she was honest enough with herself to recognize that somehow real life was slipping through her fingers. But she was unable to resist the lure of being gently led along. Although we are in less glamorous settings, many of us feel exactly as she does.

All romantic notions concerning "GOD" have a common characteristic—vagueness. While most of us do not seriously question that he exists, he is left foggily undefined. We prefer it that way. It allows us flexibility.

The last few years have seen a fantastic release of new information that has the capability of shaking our old unbelief system to its very core. In light of these new facts atheism becomes over-simplistic. The easy-out death wish of the rebel is inadequate. As we shall see in the pages to follow, such a clear profile of God is emerging in our modern world that only the truly reckless can afford to retain the vague romantic notions of him they once held.

Robert Jastrow, Director of NASA's Goddard Institute for Space Studies and an outspoken, self-acclaimed agnostic, recently admitted, "The details differ, but the essential elements in the astronomical and biblical accounts of Genesis are the same." A distinguished author and scientist, James Reid, predicted in his book *God, the Atom and the Universe* in the late 1960's that "science is preparing a surprise for mankind . . . at least for those who have doubts about the Bible and its God . . . this is an exciting thing to watch . . . the Bible has a special message for this atomic space age." His prediction is becoming remarkably true. For generations we assumed science to be on the side of the agnostic, threatening the faith of the faithful. The basis for this assumption can no longer exist.

Science no longer poses the threat to faith it once seemed to. Now, like a jet interceptor, it is equally effective whichever runway it finds itself on.

Recognizing God's true profile should now be an easy matter—except for the pressures that are working around us daily. . . .

---

[1]*Edna St. Vincent Millay.*

The Thinking Man's God

6
Fooling All of the People All of the Time

This is the day of the global brain. Properly sold, a single idea can be irrevocably implanted in millions of minds within an instant of time. The world is divided into huge cheering sections, roaring antagonisms back and forth at each other as quickly as the seed thoughts are planted. Describing the process exactly is not easy, but what surfaces is known as popular opinion. It works somewhat like artificial insemination.

The global brain allows infinite variations of thought to satisfy any number of free thinkers, but exercises a cruel uniformity when it comes to God. It resists the idea of a higher loyalty and ridicules the imposition of a higher morality. This has been one of the easy victories for the global brain because we too prefer it this way. The very thought of God poses a threat to our personal freedom. By our very nature we are set up to have our minds manipulated both above and below their threshold of awareness—and they are.

Even the most gifted minds can be victimized. Aldous Huxley, perfectly aware of the pitfalls of the human mind, traveled the spectrum from humanism to nihilism to hallucination. Ironically, he foretold his own undoing: "The victim of mind manipulation," he says in *Brave New World Revisited,*

> does not know he is a victim. To him the walls of his prison are invisible and he believes himself to be free.... With the best will in the world we cannot always be completely truthful or consistently rational. All that is in our power is to be as truthful and as rational as circumstances permit us to be.... I had motives for not wanting the world to have a meaning, consequently assumed that it had none, and was able without difficulty to find satisfying reasons for this assumption.

Dr. George Wald, another gifted mind, who developed his now famous principle "given enough time anything can happen, and will," shows how easy it is to play loosely with logic when the acceptability of God is involved. Dr. Wald, winner of the Nobel Prize in 1967, is one of the most respected men of science. His presupposition on the credibility of spontaneous generation classically demonstrates that even the disciplined mind cannot resist the incredible because it so desperately wants the luxury of believing only that which is acceptable. "I know," he says, "spontaneous generation of a living organism is impossible, yet here we are —as a result, I believe, of spontaneous generation" (*The Physics and Chemistry of Life*).

How beautifully permissive: having allowed the impossible, the possibilities become limitless. A whimsical quality to truth is that it lets itself appear to be on both sides at the same time. As beauty is in the eyes of the beholder, so is truth in the heart of the believer. The real question is, why does the heart want to believe as it does? The answer has little to do with superior reason or logic. It is mostly a part of our own personal mystique—and this personal mystique, for better or worse, largely decides our individual destiny.

More perplexing even than our reason is the mystery of the spirit within us—a spirit which seems to be in constant rebellion against the Creator. Bertrand Russell at one moment in his life felt capable of writing a book entitled *The Conquest of Happiness*. Yet in the last book he ever wrote, his own autobiography, he displayed the despair of a spirit that has shut God out of his life:

> We stand on the shore of an ocean, crying to the night and the emptiness. Sometimes a voice answers out of the darkness. But it is the voice of one drowning, and in a moment the silence returns. The world seems to be quite dreadful . . . to know people is to know their tragedy. . . .

This brilliant man who so greatly dominates 20th century thought was revealing the poverty of the soul that has turned its back on God.

Why do we insist on floundering at the feet of the great who readily admit they too have lost their way? In a universe that overwhelmingly declares the active presence of God, we strut around our tiny planet as though we were in charge, and as though the present confusion in our world were only temporary. We ignore the millions of non-chance circumstances that we live by so that we can continue to play our tragic little role of "King." In ignoring God, it is only a matter of time until unholy man builds for himself an unholy world and wakes up some morning hopelessly depressed. Good morning! Welcome to depression.

When we do give way to the possibility of God, invariably he is no more than the god of our own imagination. We forget that the possibilities are not limited by our own ability to imagine them. We insist on forcing infinite concepts through our finite funnel, then through the little key hole that is our understanding and we wonder why it doesn't all make sense.

Little wonder then that we have hang-ups about God and are confused by how he operates. By nature our first impulse is to "rearrange" him until we feel more comfortable. We find ourselves working in easy harmony with the global brain "fooling all of the people all of the time"—which only turns out to be us. The global brain isn't always subversive to our best interest, it simply doesn't always know what our best interest is.

The universal impulse for rearranging God is to leave us footloose and fancy free. This impulse is the result of a universal misunderstanding that personal sovereignty and personal liberty are inseparable—a misunderstanding as enormous as the concept of a flat earth and immeasurably more harmful. Every time you fly some friendly airline you surrender in part your sovereignty in order to keep intact your liberty. The captain is the boss. Don't touch the controls! It's better that way!

Consider this: the sovereignty of God and our personal freedom are *not* in conflict. Actually when we allow God to be sovereign we really enjoy our greatest measure of freedom.

Don't throw the idea out of your mind. It is a door opener—a first step toward personal freedom. Gaining liberty under God's sovereignty is a principle that does for our soul what gravity does for our feet!

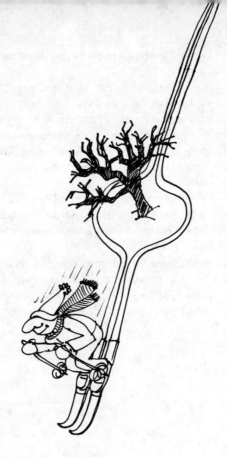

So far so good!

7
Fooling Ourselves Most of the Time

Mostly we are honest people. About the only person whom we cheat on a regular basis is ourselves, which, of course, dramatically reduces our chances of discovery!

It is said that Hitler became so abusive when he received bad news that ultimately only good news was brought to his attention. The inevitable happened—as he lost touch with reality and forced others to join in fooling him, fate closed in on him.

Some little malfunction tends to cause our integrity system to receive new information as "true" if it is friendly to opinions we already hold and "false" if it appears to challenge our more tender convictions.

The intellect can't always be relied upon to warn us against error. Instead its tendency is to fortify our opinions with logic, not because they are right, but simply because they are *ours*.

Rarely are our convictions the fruit of the intellect; much more are they the product of the whole person, his background, environment, race and culture, his personality and nature. Is black beautiful? Is white more beautiful? Everything that makes up our total personality instantly comes into play as we consider these questions. Nor can we isolate our intellect from our loyalties as words like Israeli, Palestinian, Apartheid, Lenin or Jesus drop on our ears. A whole host of associations flood in upon us with each name.

Facts are flexible, more like tools than truth. The intellect largely functions as "public relations" for the heart. This is the basic flaw in human reason and authority. This is why equally capable people can have completely opposing opinions. It is important that we recognize a principle that is continually working in everyone's life, namely that what we "see" depends largely on what we already believe. When we accept the reality of this principle working in our lives, we are bound to tread a little more warily down the garden path.

"If you hold unsound presuppositions with sufficient tenacity, facts will make no difference at all, and you will be able to create a world of your own, totally incapable of being touched by reality" (*The Altizer-Montgomery Dialogue*).

The American Indian is only so called because Columbus arrived on this continent with his mind made up that he had reached the fabled land of India. Mariner 9 has proven for all time that the so-called "canals" on Mars only exist in the eyes of the beholder.

"What we choose to see we see; this is a principle fact of our existence," says U.S. Anderson in his book, *The Magic in Your Mind!* "What we choose to believe we believe" is equally true. Circumstance forces us to live this way. Living in our physical world we can only have the tiniest idea of what is really going on all around us. Physically we are infinitesimal creatures in a sea of space and time. We are obliged to form opinions about our true nature and destiny on unimaginably incomplete information. We are the captives of our senses and only the wildest ego would speculate with any certainty beyond our sensual frontier. As far as our natural senses are concerned, we don't have any better idea of what's going on outside our own little world than does a pill in a bottle or an ant in an anthill. This, then, is the kind of unfriendly information we have to learn to handle with complete honesty if we are ever going to have any real understanding of God. If we are more than material entities we desperately need outer source data to direct us.

But what within us is able to respond to awareness beyond us? To what dangers may we be exposing ourselves, or to what rewards? We have our emotions from which, fortunately, we are unable to separate ourselves, but we are warned that these are the most primitive of tools and are too sensitive to our desires. We have reason, but it has no access to facts beyond our senses. And we are left then with only our imagination or intuition. Somewhere deep within us, like the spokes of a wheel all starting to turn at once, are our reason, imagination, intuition and emotion shaping our perceptions, forming our presuppositions, then coming forth as our opinions.

Without a reliable supernatural extension of our senses, we are adrift in a world of pure fancy, and we will have no trouble finding the facts needed to suit that fancy. What this means is that with the data which is on hand, or which is ever likely to be, we simply do not have the input to rule out the alternative of God —or the hope that we can come into a mature understanding of him.

The pill in the bottle lacks a dimension that we fortunately have, but unfortunately largely neglect—our spirit! This reliable supernatural extension to our senses will save us from living in a world of pure fancy. It does not function on the "see and believe," or "show me" principle as do our senses. It functions on "the believe and then you shall see" principle. Nobody would ever dream of insisting on breathing through their ear, and if they did, they would bound to suffocate. It is all too obvious that the ear simply was never intended for that purpose! Neither were the senses intended to search for God. Our spirit, by faith—which is "the believe and see" principle at work—must do the reaching out. The new outlook must come to us through our spirit. So, really quite contrary to popular opinion, the *best* of the better options is still open to us—discovering that God is real and learning to live in exciting harmony with him. Once the very best option is ours, it's hard to believe the difference it makes in living!

As we learn to listen to our spirit, we become more

conscious of a Presence—a Presence to which just a little while ago we never gave a second thought. Our minds were sealed like a vault against him for reasons now we can't even recall. The more intimately we identify with him, the less restless we are in our souls. This is called the second look! For many of us it won't happen that easily. Our hang-ups keep getting in the way. But the stakes are too high and eternity far too long to have a future that hangs on a snap decision!

Was Dr. George Wald, renowned scientist, Higgins Professor of Biology at Harvard and Nobel Prize Winner in 1967, whom we quoted earlier as believing in the incredible probabilities of chance creation, indulging himself in a second look when he pleaded with his academic peers at a symposium on "Science & the Social Imperatives":

> The only way the world is going to stop short of the brink of nuclear holocaust is a return to God and the principles of the Bible. Nuclear holocaust can be averted by faith, love, and hope, and the precious principles of the Bible. I know that this is the sheerest, non-academic sentimentality, but I am convinced that this is the only way . . .

Given enough time . . .

8
Footsteps!

If you suddenly stumbled upon it all, what would you think? There, floating into your vision, different from all the dead and arid balls that you have seen before, is Earth, breathlessly beautiful. In the midst of the desolate space, a treasure world of life and color passes before your eyes. Its lakes and rivers and oceans teem with fish. The magic sprinkling of earth is full of seeds. Trees hang heavy with fruit and no deeper below the earth's surface than the meat beneath an orange skin lie oil and coal and iron and gold. There is water enough to nourish the earth and satisfy our thirst. It is a home alone in space, its cupboards once filled with all the good things that would ever be needed.

When Goldilocks stumbled into the little cottage deep in the forest, the porridge was warm, the table was set, and the beds were turned down. In the uncomplicated mind of a little girl it meant someone must be near. And she was right. As she listened she heard footsteps coming through the door. Surely it is impossible to enjoy the fruits of the earth and not be conscious of Footsteps.

Are we, then, just a spin-off of the universe or should we be listening for footsteps? Should the prospect be frightening—or comforting? These are the questions that defy an impartial answer. High quality reasoning can have it either way. Without intellectual embarrassment we are free to believe as we wish. Remember, our first impulse is to allow our integrity system to malfunction, and discredit as unfriendly information any hint that out there somewhere is an authority to be reckoned with. Don't let it happen! Don't assume right off that we need to be afraid of the footsteps. *They could be friendly!* This time let's be our own persons. Let's not be manipulated by popular opinion. Let's first decide if it is reasonable to expect footsteps—later we can decide whether they are likely to be friendly.

The Science Year Book of Encyclopedia Britannica has this to say on the subject of spin-offs and the chance of any recognizeable pattern emerging out of them:

> One would have to wait, on the average, many million times the "age" of the universe before 100 particles in an otherwise empty shoe box would gather, say, in the left half of the box, just by chance

of their random motions. This spontaneous display of organization is so unlikely that it is practically impossible. But a degree of organization that is immensely less probable, such as the arrangement of 10^{25} particles into a functioning chipmunk, does happen every time a chipmunk is conceived and born.

H. Dingle, in the British *Journal for the Philosophy of Science,* makes this observation:

The view that all . . . happenings have a definite probability . . . of being realized . . . cannot be disproved. Nevertheless, I doubt in his heart of hearts anyone believes it. It implies that . . . if we continue for an indefinite time to put kettles of water on the fire, it is certain that the water in one of them will freeze. My own conviction is that it never would occur. It is more probable that the scheme which requires it is wrong.

Dr. Howard Holroyd, discussing the infinitesimal probability of design by chance, adds this additional thought:

Making things worse requires no imagination, no research, no insight, no mathematics; all that is required to obtain worse design is to change things in a random manner. To reach perfection is indeed difficult, but imperfection can be reached without effort (Creation Research Society).

Briefly this is the question we must ask in our second look: If we stand in the midst of our world which is so vast and complex, yet so individually unique that we will never end recording it, let alone understand it, can it best be explained by chance—or by plan?

Our second look must begin at the beginning when there was absolutely nothing at all. Out of this absolute void the basic elements of creation began to appear in the most intricate designs and varieties. Mysteriously, like popcorn, some of these elements starting popping into life, conscious and unconscious, into myriad shapes and sizes, habits and instincts, so unique no one will ever write "Finis" to their cataloging.

How it happened nobody will ever know. It was not "observed" then, nor is the process being observed now. Everybody's faith must start with a miracle. There is no way around it—it has to be a miracle of chance or a miracle through intelligence. Sir John Eccles, winner of the Nobel prize in Science, has estimated that the probability of life having happened solely by chance just once in the past is 400,000 trillion, trillion, trillion to one. A more recent reading of computer science concludes that creation by chance is so mathematically improbable as to be impossible.

If we are beginning to think Randomness, Selection and Time leave something to be desired, we don't really have to feel suddenly exposed. We can immediately substitute for it the highly intriguing principle of Intelligence, Method and Time. The more we let ourselves think about it, the more delightful its possibilities become. We can easily identify with it because it is working around us every day. A superior intelligence using superior methods naturally does things more quickly—like television replacing smoke signals and the outboard motor replacing the raft. The extension of this principle is that supernatural Intelligence using supernatural methods can do things instantly.

A hundred years ago it took several weeks for a voice to cross the ocean. Today, thanks to superior intelligence and technology, we can engage in instant conversation. All this time we have been living with the unfortunate mental hang-up "that things which seem too incredible to happen quickly become more believable if only they happen slowly enough."

Instant man, instant trees, instant rocks and instant oceans brought into being by a Higher Intelligence seems like a much better bet than just leaving the parts lying around waiting for something to happen! There is not a reason in the world why instant man didn't come with a navel, trees with their annual rings, and rocks with their radio-active clocks set at noon or even later.

So—why God? Because the only other alternative has become incredibly unlikely! But there is also another very good reason. Deep down inside each of us we have always known he was there, if we would only let ourselves admit it. As far back as our search can go, we have always believed in God. We have always had a deeply religious nature. The scratchings on caves and the litter of tombs, legends and myths, songs, dances, odes —every way that man has to express the yearnings of his soul reveals he has always known there was a God.

In *Modern Man in Search of his Soul,* Dr. Carl Jung says:

> The human psyche from time immemorial has been shot through with religious feelings and ideas. Whoever cannot see this is blind, and whoever chooses to explain it away . . . has no sense of reality. . . . If we do not acknowledge the idea of God consciously, something else is made God.

Samuel Miller in his book, *Are You Nobody?,* says,

> Believing is as much an integral factor in man as eating and sleeping. He neither gains nor loses faith; he merely changes the object of it. There is little or nothing that man will not believe. Man is simply an inveterate, incurable, inevitable believer.

With such a background behind us, no wonder Dr. Paul Tournier says the great state of world neurosis stems from denying the reality of God. We are denying an essential need within ourselves.

Yes—we *should* expect to hear footsteps! Logic certainly seems to say so. Our deepest instincts confirm it and our peace of mind demands it. The most pressing question then emerges—when we hear the footsteps, how friendly will they turn out to be?

9

The Footsteps
are Friendly!

A short while ago an old fellow was released from prison after serving over forty years of his sentence. After a few days he returned to his jail cell voluntarily—he couldn't stand the freedom! A major hang-up for many of us is thinking that once we accept the reality of God we end our days of freedom. We have yet to discover that coming into a true experience with him is a staggering release into freedom. Anyone who loves freedom can love God! We have no reason to hold him at arm's length in fear he will limit our freedom. Turning him off on the basis of lost freedom is like the old fellow refusing to come out of his cell.

Consider the tyranny that we subject ourselves to if

we accept the principle of "life by chance." We are hopelessly locked into a mindless parade of atoms. We can never escape the cycle of death we see all around us. We are in total bondage to the laws of nature with nothing of our individuality surviving except our memoirs. Such dismal, unexciting, meaningless concepts have given birth to the cry of absurdity. Nihilism is embraced as a blessed release. People just keep recycling like radishes.

Maybe we don't wake up in the morning worrying about this and the futility of it we may be able to endure, but the real tragedy of "life by chance" is that it is not even a valid option. The God of the Bible tells us that 5000 years from now each of us will be alive somewhere—the only real question is where? Yet "life by chance" leaves us with *nothing,* so it is not even one of the better of the bad options. As an option it doesn't even exist. Life by chance is no chance at all. It is not the intellectual alternative to God—it is not even an alternative.

Within the last few years our minds have been offered a release from the depressing implications of three dimensional tyranny. The science of relativity has swept us into a multi-dimensional universe. It encourages us to believe we are no longer terminal. Something about us is truly eternal. For those who are paying attention it is proving to be an exhilarating experience. Blinds are going up, windows are being thrown open, and a growing throng of us are stepping into the bright sunshine. We are becoming aware that in the eternal riddle we are something special.

Relativity's message reinforces the fact that we have

been led down the garden path. We have been made prisoners of our own physical senses. The *real* world lies somewhere beyond this one and we are surely a part of it. Our world is not a world of annihilation but one of transformation. There is no extinction. We are not confined by absolutes of time, motion or space.

Einstein refined the theory that time and mass are both relative. We have long been subdued by our relative physical insignificance in this universe. A life, like a momentary spark in light years of time, seemed barely worthwhile. Then with the dawn of relativity, we confront the great possibility that whomever, whatever we are, we are deathless. The real stuff that is *us* is endless. Overflowing the *natural,* we are of the *supernatural.* The key to our significance is not length of bone, but life—endless conscious life. Each of us is not, after all, a speck on a speck in an ocean of space, but a unique living personality in an eternity of time. What a difference this makes!

Martin Gardner, in his book *Relativity for the Millions,* writes: "There are thousands of scientists (including physicists) who have as much difficulty understanding the basic concepts of relativity as a child has in understanding why the people of China do not fall off the earth."

James Reid says in the book *God, the Atom, and the Universe* that the implications of the real world of relativity only began to be recognized within the last ten years. "The universe is even stranger than our fantasies," states astrophysicist Jesse Greenstein of Hale Observatories. Small wonder that J. B. S. Haldane, the late great British scientist, could say,

"The universe is not only queerer than we suppose, but queerer than we *can* suppose." Isn't this an open invitation for us to extend our understanding of who we really are?

A sixth sense has continually told us of a world beyond this skin. We are about to receive the full impact of the fact that physical death is not the ultimate disaster. Is it dawning on you yet? The world that relativity is pointing to is the same world the Bible revealed to us so long ago.

This brings to mind the story of the good Indian scout who acquired uncanny skill to follow a trail impossible for the normal eye to detect. It was impossible however, to get ahead of the trail without coming face to face with its maker—and beyond the maker there was no trail! Science at its best can only follow its Maker's trail. Beyond the Maker there is no trail. The science of relativity is a pursuit of the highest order.

In a very meaningful way the Bible makes an analogy between God and light that is both exquisitely simple and infinitely profound. "God is light and in him is no darkness at all." (1 John 1:5)

On the subject of light science has established the following theories:

"At the speed of light an object in size is reduced to zero."

"At the speed of light mass becomes infinite."

"At the speed of light time stands still."

Think about it. Could any other analogy define so beautifully an invisible, omnipresent, eternal God? Slowly we realize the "ups" and "downs" and the "risings" and "settings" of the Bible can no longer be considered unfortunate references of a pre-scientific period. Relativity says there are no absolute "ups" and "downs" in interstellar space because there is no available frame of reference. Heaven can be "up" and hell can be "down" whether you live in Toronto or Hong Kong. When the frame of reference is the earth, speaking of the "rising sun" is not an error or even an indiscretion. Do the heavens revolve or does the earth rotate? Martin Gardner says this question is meaningless. A waitress might just as sensibly ask a customer if he wants his ice cream on top of his pie or his pie under his ice cream. If tomorrow morning when we wake up, the entire universe, including ourselves, has increased or decreased in size ten times, no one will ever know or even become suspicious.

Historians claim that in time of crisis people turn to the supernatural. It probably is more accurate to say that as people run out of gas, they look beyond themselves. Our society is no different. We are in the middle of crisis. Almost every environmental alarm is set to go off around the year 2000. Scientists and environmentalists tell us the world will then be running out of everything. Everything but people. And our anxiety over this is slowly breaking down our hang-ups about the supernatural.

As our hang-ups break down we seriously begin to reappraise the so-called "human phenomenon." We hear impressive phrases like "man is an insoluble puzzle. . . . an incomprehensible wonder. . . . an object of abiding perplexity." Not to be outdone, John Doe exclaims, "There is more to man than you can hit with a stick." This is his way of saying that man has a supernatural dimension and that therefore there may well be a supernatural solution to our problems.

Why the God of the Bible? Because he has never spoken more clearly than he is doing today—and we should be listening. He *is* real. He *is* credible. He *is* personal. And we should be bringing our lives into harmony with the fact of his being.

It is time to throw away our hang-ups about him. All the evidence around us says the time has come to release our spirits by faith and reach out to him. The ground rules are simple—we use them everyday: "Believe and see":

"For he that would come to God must believe that he is." (Hebrews 11:6)

"Believe and you shall see the glory of God." (John 11:40) Don't hold back!

The concept that we are not alone in the universe is becoming increasingly popular. We have an uncomfortable feeling that we are being "observed". Pioneer 10 is rocketing through the heavens with man's message to whomever may be out there. Powerful radio telescopes are scanning trillions of stars in genuine anticipation of discovery. With all this display of credibility that someone *is* out there, why not bow to the weight of evidence and say that Someone is God? The indications are that he is friendly!

"He's a hard bargainer—he'll give us the milk and honey, but the anti-adultery clause stays in."

10
O God, Have A Heart!

Probably the most universal hang-up about God is his seeming indifference to suffering. Every time you pick up your newspaper or turn on your T.V., there it is again—somewhere, somebody is hurting.

"A desperate, destitute little family of four threw themselves under the wheels of an onrushing train. Their screams were lost in the roar of the wheels. . . ."

"Aimlessly, a teenage mother wanders down an inner city street populated by old, drunken men and hungry, dirty children. Grasping her breast, an emaciated child sucks nourishment from a body that can hardly keep itself alive. The rags she wears expose bare buttocks to an insensitive, staring world. . . ."

"A sidewalk is home. The ditch is the bathroom. Two bricks are the stove. The only fuel is cow dung. A dead crow is supper for the man and woman and their three small children. . . ."

"Like ants struggling with loads twice their size, the long lines of people plod on. Nameless and faceless, clutching all their worldly possessions, they flee from bombed and burning villages, from nothing to nothing, chased by fear to already overcrowded refugee camps. The unending trek of throw-away people increases. . . ."

"Soldiers became pallbearers, protecting themselves from infection by wearing rubber gloves and masks. As they laid the 100 dark coffins in the trench, the earth beneath their feet still trembled in aftershock. An unknown number of bodies still lay like broken dolls buried in the debris. A weary priest slowly shook his head. "Nobody prayed," he said. "They don't believe a God could be so cruel. . . . I don't believe it either."

"Suddenly a car swerved into the oncoming lane. The long screeching of tires was followed by an explosion of metal. Screams of terror filled the air and flames quickly enveloped the little faces pressed against the windows."

Everywhere—around the corner and across the ocean—misery, pain and fear grow in overwhelming proportions. And lately something new and ominous is stirring around us. Terrorists are searching out the innocent for hostage, ransom, and destruction.

O God, have a heart! Doesn't it move you to tears when you look down and see how your children are hurting? Why do you allow it to go on? Some say you couldn't stop it if you would. Others say you wouldn't stop it if you could. How can you say you care and yet let these things happen? Maybe you're not even there!

Of course, we have every right to honestly ask these questions! But having asked them, it's only fair that we stay around for the answers. By erasing the very thought of God in our anger or frustration, we do not in any way eliminate the problem, just the only possible hope of a solution. The problem of suffering can never disprove God. It can only suggest that he is cruel or indifferent. If God *is* the heartless tyrant many think him to be, then there is much to recommend that we become friendly with him.

Deny him or defy him! Whatever our inclination may be, neither gives understanding or relief to suffering. Yes, it is only human to blame God when we are hurting. After all, who's in charge here anyway? And as the cries rise up to a seemingly empty sky it is easy to believe God is busy someplace else in his universe and isn't doing much to help.

It is here, with this problem of suffering, that our second look meets its biggest challenge. Pain and suffering are our major accusations against God. Mentally we have fortified ourselves against him on this issue. Even now our presuppositions may not allow us a fair second look. But if we are satisfied the footsteps are friendly and our personal freedom is not threatened, then any *real* solution to suffering should come as friendly information. Agreed?

In fairness to God, let's concede one thing. When we're hurting is when he gets our best, and often our only, attention. Suffering for some reason acts like a magnet drawing us toward him. All along God has been obliged to contend with a long standing human paradox. It is a perversity we indulge ourselves in: the afflicted seek him, the affluent neglect him. The Bible describes it this way:

> "Then at last, when he had ruined them . . . how earnestly they turned around and followed him!" (Psalm 78:34, TLB)

An employee at a local refinery experienced a complete loss of his sense of feeling. One day while standing inside a pressure vessel steaming it down, he boiled the soles of his feet without any discomfort. Rather than fire him, the management moved him to inside shopwork. Not much later however, while working on a grinder, he noticed blood on the wheel—his first indication that he was working on his own finger!

Just as pain is the early warning signal for sickness and injury, so suffering is an ever present warning of sin. In an idealistic world where no one could suffer, war could easily go on forever. Why would anyone want to stop it? Hate could express itself quite freely. Random rape could become a harmless pastime. Drinking oneself into the jolly tremors could even be fun. And when all our homes and our souls lie in ashes, who's been hurt? So, human nature being what it is, let's enjoy the luxury of suffering a bit. Without it sin would know no bounds!

Sin and suffering are inseparable. If there was no sin there would be no suffering. The theological heavies knock themselves out on this relationship. But God has spoken very clearly on this matter:

> "When Adam sinned, sin entered the entire human race. His sin spread death throughout all the world, so everything began to grow old and die, for all sinned." (Romans 5:12, TLB)

Let's get the blame where it belongs. It will help our understanding. We can see this principle at work all around us today. Our generation is suffering because of the dumb choices and mistakes our parents have made. And tomorrow's children will suffer from our mistakes.

Having a positive attitude toward suffering is another step in the right direction. Suffering is a fact of life. We can never escape it. It is bound to touch our lives sooner or later. Far more important than explaining why we suffer is finding out how to handle it successfully when it arrives—and our options are limited.

As a matter of fact, we have only four options. We discover the first two when we seek consolation in the mysticism of the East—learn to accept it! or learn to ignore it! A third way to handle suffering is to rationalize it! The humanist of the western world seeks his comfort in this way. And if you are keeping up to date on the situation, you will recognize him by his attitude of bitterness and despair. Suffering is so much harder to endure when it has no apparent purpose.

The fourth option is to overcome it!

"In this world you will have troubles, but be of good

cheer, I have overcome the world." (John 16:33)
"Who is he that overcomes the world, but he that
believes that Jesus is the Son of God." (1 John 5:5)

Meeting our problems in his strength is no wild-
eyed theory. You can test it every day of the week. The
human paradox works all around us, proving again
and again that man's adversity is God's opportunity
and more often than not it is the only one he gets.

Far more praise to God comes from prisons than
penthouses. Prayers of thanksgiving are always more
sincere over hard won bread than lobster tails. This
is just our nature, and who would know better than
God, our Creator. It's always the same. More love for
God is expressed from wheelchairs than armchairs.
Greater victories have been won beside a grave than
on any football field. God meets us at our point of
need. When we have a need too big to handle ourselves he meets us there. It's the sweetest kind of victory. In this paradox the human spirit overcomes the
groanings of the flesh. For many, the most moving
moment of their lives has been Jesus glimpsed for the
first time through tears.

Any day of the week you can visit Jerry in his wheelchair, bitter and lonely. One of the first things he will
say to you is, "God put me here." Life for him is over,
and as far as he is concerned, the sooner the pretense
of it is finished, the better.

The same day of the week you can visit George. He
too lives in a wheelchair. He also operates his own
business. He is so enthusiastic about what God has in
store for him and he knows the wheelchair and the

twisted body are only temporary inconveniences.

Or you can speak to Ted. Daily he fights for his breath and continually is being rushed to the emergency room for life-giving respiration. Yet he will say and mean with all his heart, "I wouldn't have missed those days in intensive care for anything." It was then that God blessed his spirit in a special way and met him in his need.

What George and Ted have is far more than just the ability to handle suffering—it is enthusiasm for the person with whom they are really supposed to be angry. Maybe we should take another look at them! Jesus bearing his cross and loving Ted we have come to accept. But Ted bearing his cross and loving Jesus, humanly speaking, is harder to explain. Human frailty is being brought into a special place of fellowship.

As we watch George and Ted and so many more like them, we begin to lose the resentment we once had for Divine indifference. In our bitterness toward what seems like senseless suffering, we have failed to see that in the pain something utterly precious is emerging—a priceless demonstration of unconditional love. It is the cry of Job rising up over and over again, "Though he slay me, still I will trust in him." (Job 13:15) The more we observe of this love, the easier the things we still don't understand rest upon our hearts. Of course, much about suffering we find hard to explain, and we would choose no part of suffering our ourselves, but it reveals the wonder of Jesus "living in us" apparent in no other way.

Suffering is going to be with us as long as this world goes on. Can you really think of any life that has avoided its touch completely? Each person's life plan should include the possibility of suffering. Poor Pam was so convinced that the sure way to learn was from mistakes. But isn't it a shame to overlook men like George and Ted and not learn also from them what really works!

O God, have a heart! Such a cry born of deep despair does not offend God. So very often it is the first time some lips have meaningfully formed his name:

> "And God who is rich in mercy, who has such love for us, as he has so longed to do, lifts us into heavenly places with Christ Jesus, and over the ages to come will show us the exceeding riches of his grace . . . our present sufferings are not worth comparing with the glory that will be revealed in us." (Ephesians 2:4-7, Romans 8:18)

Once we can see above our troubles and the troubles surrounding us, nothing works such a remarkable personality transformation on us as being caught up in the delights of all the things that God is doing *right!*

"Whadda ya mean, I'm lost!"

11
The Long Arm of Love

Have you ever seen blind, quiet hate in the eyes of a man—the kind of hate that will endure any hardship, pay any price, and if necessary wait forever to search out and destroy? Hate arranges its own meeting place. A few years ago at the Munich Olympics, hate, fear and pride, or some combination of all these passions, came together to search out and destroy. Although cause and place vary, this manifestation of hate has become almost a daily happening.

The genius of nature seems to have no limit for arranging times and meeting places around us continually. A biologist at a remote station in the upper reaches of the Fraser River watches a salmon that has fought its way thousands of ocean and river-miles, probing the very water spout it dropped through as a fingerling. A hawk swoops down on a bluejay with a shuddering squawk as their bodies collide in mid air.

Two people obviously only in their late teens pull up to a second rate motel and register as man and wife. Call it lust or love, whatever it is, it too has its meeting place. There is no end. Our earth abounds with single minded drives that bring us into destiny-changing relationships.

Love can be as intense as hate, if not more so. No price is too high to pay, no suffering too great to endure, no end of the earth too far to search to find its meeting place. Love can also have its place of parting, beside a grave, or sometimes even in a hotel room . . .

Early one morning love came to an end in a hotel room in Mexico City. Only voices, a man's and a woman's, came through the thin walls. She was heartbroken, pleading and weeping, looking for any hope. His voice was low, detached, unloving. He didn't even bother answering her questions. It was over. You could feel the death of love through the walls. She waited for one last word that might hold things together. It never came. The door closed and you could hear her steps as she walked to the lobby. Thousands of miles from home, in the middle of a vacation, about 3 A.M., a dying love finally ended.

God is also in the business of searching out his meeting place. Being God, all the options are his—fear, coercion, instinct, or some form of divine hypnosis. He chooses to use love. "You will find me" he says, "when you search for me with all your *heart*." (Jeremiah 29:13) He willingly makes his love known—to be returned or trampled as we see fit. He waits until we can return it freely, and when we do there is no good-bye beside a grave or hollow hotel scene—there is no parting.

To trust God we no longer need to have all the answers. We do not have to enter into all his mysteries. Even if such an all-knowing love could exist in us, it would delay our meeting place with God forever. He is simply too vast for our comprehension. The heart is the heart and it is made to love without understanding. We love our earthly father long before we have any idea how he puts bread on the table. We eagerly reach out to him from our crib for no other reason than that he is our father. This kind of love from us is what our heavenly Father waits for.

Reaching up to a seemingly empty sky is not a blind act of faith. When you reach up to him with all your heart, he's there. It's an absolute certainty. It was planned that way long before the world ever was. Before the first man ever lost his way, God's search and rescue operation was ready. It is the work of the Spirit, the Wind of God. He is God's long arm of love reaching from as far as heaven may be into the most distant corners of the earth.

The way of the wind is a fascinating display of sovereign power. It can spread itself across a meadow, touching flowers here and there, leaving others motionless as it passes them by. It can cause a slender stem to sway gently, or snap a giant cedar as if it were a twig. It can suddenly sweep from overhead and move low hanging clouds to reveal the beauty of the sun. Unseen and unsearchable, the Spirit, as the wind, moves where he will. Wherever he goes and whatever he touches springs into new life. This interaction is called "being born of the Spirit."

How does the Spirit work? In different, mysterious ways. . . . A Moslem in the Red Sea area was reading the Koran. Somehow as he read about Jesus it came to him that this Jesus seemed more important even than Mohammed. He decided he should pray to Allah, in the name of Jesus. A short time later he saw a man in a vision standing beside him with scars in the palms of his hands. The mystery of who this man was remained until sometime later when he heard a missionary telling about the cross.

Before a missionary left Hong Kong to go into a remote inland area, he purchased a new sweater to take with him. As he neared the distant village an old man sitting outside the community addressed him, "You have a message I have been waiting for all these years. I recognize you by your sweater." These instances are true and the characters, except possibly the old man, are living today. Unusual? Unlikely? It is the way of the Wind! The unusual and the unlikely are only ordinary to him.

In both the remotest of places and right before our eyes, slender stems and giant cedars are moving under the sovereign power of the Wind of God. None are missed who do not wish to be missed. Maybe we are beginning to see a value system at work that the world knows nothing about. It is spelling out loudly and clearly the most urgent of messages to every earth dweller—God loves! Souls have no color, and to God the somebodies and the nobodies are all the same! He loves the anybodies everywhere and anywhere.

From the moment when God allowed his very heart to be nailed to a tree, there has never been any doubt of his love. His action gives the lie to those who tear the world apart, then blame it all on him. It is his assurance that when the innocent suffer he is able to empathize. It is his guarantee that he has not forsaken us in the midst of a world seemingly gone mad. He is open to the most feeble of whispers:

"God, if you are, whoever you are, speak to me."

This cry of the human spirit to the Unknown reveals a touch by the Wind. God has responded to each man's cry even before it is spoken. This guiding system is far superior to the one in the pea-sized brain of the salmon! It is the first stirring of love in some human heart toward God. The Wind is about to whisper in still another ear the truth about Jesus. The long arm of God's love is arranging another meeting place!

12
Gone With The Wind

Inevitably the house lights come on. The magic spell breaks, and minds grudgingly begin adjusting back to reality. People slowly move toward the aisles, tramping underfoot the litter of paper cups and candy wrappers; then they begin shuffling awkwardly uphill to the lobby. Once outside, mingling with the crowd and exposed again to the noise of the streets, the lingering make-believe world quickly evaporates.

The projectionist deftly rewinds the film and once again returns it to its metal container. It looks just as uninteresting as any other metal container. No one seeing it would suspect how easily its contents can take our minds and hearts and make them live entranced in another day and world, appealing, attractive and plastic.

But it will happen again and again. With the slow spin of the reel, Rhett Butler will suddenly come alive before us. He will draw us headlong into his romantic world with his reckless, devil-may-care manner. And Scarlett will emerge, selfish, beautiful, impulsive, but ever so alive. All the charm of the Deep South with its passion for courage and honor will penetrate into our thoughts, and the swelling music will command our moods through scenes of victory, defeat and heart-break. This bright world so easily outshines the dreari-ness of our own lives that we want to keep the nostalgia around us as a delightful interlude for days. But all the glitter is just another romantic page out of history, gone with the wind, to be replayed again and again— but never again to be relived.

Even now we can recreate in our own minds vibrant, real personalities we once knew and their very memory pulls on our emotions. They too are gone with the wind, silent, committed to history, waiting. But God has ar-ranged a time for every life to come before him —not by the slow turning of a reel, but alive and in his presence. Jesus, before he ascended, left us this message:

> "I tell you this, that you must give account on judg-ment day for every idle word you speak. Your words now reflect your fate then: either you will be justified by them or you will be condemned." (Matthew 12:36, 37 TLB)

That sounds fair enough! But how does he plan on doing it?

Maybe Dr. Wilder Penfield, foremost researcher of the human brain, has given us the key. In an interview with *Maclean's,* Canada's National Magazine, he said, "The brain unconsciously hoards each detail of every hour—playback can be elicited by electrical stimuli. I can see clearly the brain is a computer, the most wonderful computer in existence . . . computed by something outside itself—the mind." Will we relive our lives before God in technicolor? What an unnerving thought! Not just a reel taken from its metal container, but a real life raised up from the grave, alive again, bringing with it its little computer, with every idle thought and word safely recorded. One day each of our epitaphs too will read, "Gone with the Wind" . . . but only for awhile!

Once again we must confront all the mystery of the whereabouts of dear old Bill and what his end might be. Did he ever hear footsteps? Did he discover the love of God—or did he trifle with it too long? Only the technicolor replay will tell the tale.

Endangered species?

13
The Kiss of Death

It happens in many ways. We may have already received it and not know it. The kiss of death is a real possibility and lasts for as long as forever is. There are many tell-tale signs that will let us know if we have received this fatal embrace even when to all outward appearances we have everything all nicely put together. One sign, however, is more noticeable than all the others.

One of the great personalities of romantic fictional literature spent his entire career masquerading in one disguise or another, but he was always easily found out. No matter how clever the disguise, sooner or later he gave himself away. He had the peculiar mannerism of drumming his fingers on the table top.

As clever as Satan is, he too has a peculiar mannerism. It was never more evident than at the cross. He must have known Christ's certain victory over evil would seal his doom, and yet we read just before Jesus' betrayal, "Then Satan entered into Judas." (Luke 22:3) He was exhibiting the peculiar mannerism that has always revealed his presence—self destruction. It is basic to his nature to tear down, to destroy. It's so basic to him he can't even make an exception of himself. He siezes every opportunity to invade people's lives, and then, slowly but surely, you can see them begin to self destruct. They have received the kiss of death.

Karl Menninger was probably not aware of the profound principle of human nature he uncovered when he wrote in his book *Man Against Himself,* "It is true, in the end each man kills himself in his own selected way. There are so many occasions to witness it before our eyes. The methods are legion. . . . This is the true evidence of a spiritual malignancy within us." The ability of human genius to produce is only surpassed by the capacity of human nature to destroy.

Satan is deceptively invisible. He maintains a very low profile, but like a master poltergeist he makes his presence known. When you see people behaving in an erotic and abandoned manner, ignoring all the normal instincts for personal survival, when you see lives fall and shatter like thrown pieces of crockery, you can be sure that Satan is somewhere near.

Even though he can be easily discovered, Satan has always been the superb impersonator. He is a tireless and convincing performer, but underneath is still the same old actor with the same old act. Only the cast and the scenario keep changing. Satan easily identifies himself with blue denim and bracing western air or with streams cascading down the mountainside. Yet he is equally at home in the elegant club, so elegant that most of us would be flattered to even know the waiter. He is very much at ease with the hazel-eyed model lounging wherever, in whatever, lending her undeniable appeal to the choicest bourbon in the land. City sophisticate or back-to-earth woodsman, young or old, rich or poor—he's comfortable with anyone, anywhere, anytime. But after each scene in his play, backstage becomes a dumping ground for the debris of broken lives. The master poltergeist is at work.

More and more young people are being caught up in Satan's wreckage. The story is too heartbreaking to tell, and parents sit home stunned, wondering where they went wrong. . . .

"She was only 18, working as a stenographer in a downtown office. They picked her up leaning helplessly against a telephone pole. A skid row bum had just kicked her out of his room because she was too spaced out and rubbery-legged for his bed. After working for a few more days, she disappeared again. . . ." Changing only a few details, this becomes an every day story, and the kids in it are sixteen, fifteen and often younger.

"Oh please Mr. Satan, have a heart!" Go ahead and cry. He's not about to pay any attention to you. And besides, nobody really holds anything against him anyway. He keeps on playing to "standing room only audiences'" . . . and really his show *does* look like fun— except for those on the outer edges of the crowd who thrash around in self destruction. The show goes on and the big time, all time loser pours his peculiar mannerism into still another life. But every once in awhile a voice will cry, "O God, why don't *you* do something?" . . . and if the cry is truly a cry and not a curse, God will pour out assurance from his Word:

> "For God loved the world so much that he gave his only Son so that anyone who believes in him shall not perish but have eternal life." (John 3:16, TLB)

Such is the heart of God. His solution to the kiss of death is the love of Jesus—and Jesus has always been more readily available than dope or cheap sex or a three martini lunch!

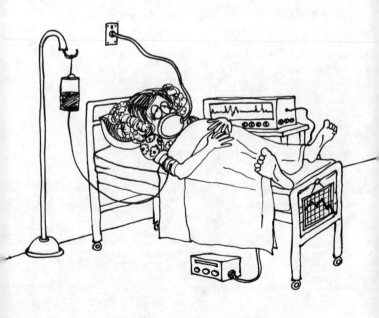

"Like I was saying . . . I have no need."

14
The Lonely Act

What's ahead? More specifically, what's ahead for
"*me*"? Well, for one thing there's a cloud in our future
—death—and it's the ultimate hang-up! How we handle it is the final test of our integrity system's relia-
bility. This time it's playing for keeps!

Vance Packard's recent book, *The People Shapers*,
says that our on-rushing technology has given our generation the most precarious place in human history.
Through technology we have acquired the chilling
ability to play God. Soon we will have the capability
of producing either "perfect man" or "manimals."
Human engineers will now be able to plan a new future
for us with *human* nature deciding what our new

nature should be. The results should be devastating! The philosophy behind it is that "the soul is no more than an invention of earlier, deluded, less informed times." It seems we possess infinite plasticity and whenever it seems desirable, we easily can be "dehumanized." On first reading, and even second, the impression one gets is that man is fashioning what he believes to be his final escape from God. B. F. Skinner holds out this hope for us: "We have not yet seen what man can make of man." I'll bet you can hardly wait!

Unfortunately, time for many of us is not a luxury. The People Shapers are misreading the problem. We are reasonably happy people as we are. It is the cloud in our future that is bothering us. The solution isn't found in tinkering with a plan that will let us live to be one hundred. What we want is good advice that will let us live forever—and most everyone has an uncomfortable feeling that the here and now has some bearing on that possibility.

The little old lady peering into the coffin of her recently departed husband was heard to say, "The shell is there but the nut is gone." Most of us are prepared to admit that dear old grandma spoke some truth. She expressed our suspicion that sooner or later we are obliged to set out on a mysterious and often poorly defined pathway.

This gnawing suspicion all begins as we find ourselves standing on the outer rim of a glittering world teeming with that magic substance called "life." Our little hearts begin to beat with excitement! We want to become a part of it all! Call it acceptance or recognition—we all love it. It's a longing the heart will never lose. Sometimes it seems there is no price too high to pay for the feeling that we really *belong*. The fear of being alone never leaves us . . . and on this hangs much of the story of life.

Little people, hungry for attention, will press the details of their lives the clerk in the store or the person next to them on the bus when given even the slightest encouragement. Even important people struggle to impress. They never give up trying to wring some special recognition from the maitre d' or even from the bell boy as they stand alone with him in the elevator. The "big wheel" is having his acceptance problems too. Some of the finest performances are played around a lonely beer, when the bartender shows only a casual interest in our tiny worlds. We sit alone with a studied demeanor, playing to an audience that has forgotten us before our backs are out the door. Even the tiniest ego struggles to expand the importance of its role.

It will always be this way. The nomadic soul is trying to find its way home. But *here* is not its home. Every soul is transient, it is only passing through. A time of parting comes in every relationship, no matter how tender or how special. We have no roots, no permanency—everything is temporary. We live an airport experience of endless passing faces. We are the vagabonds of the universe without acceptance or recognition, slipping back to the outer rim, and then beyond. Life is a lonely act.

But the scene is being set for the loneliest act of all. Except for a few close relatives and friends, the audiences we have played to along the way have mostly been an illusion. But despite anything our loved ones can do, our three biggest scenes we play alone; coming, going, and standing before God. But really this doesn't have to be the loneliest act. . . .

A little while ago I watched a gallant old gentleman die—my father. As he lay there on his bed he didn't seem to be a vagrant soul at all. It became obvious to us watching that we were not a part of what was going on. During those last few hours when his eyes were closed, he would smile and occasionally through his dry and parted lips we would hear a chuckle. Every so often, as I sat there beside him, I could hear him softly say, "Jesus! Jesus!" Slowly he was slipping toward the outer rim, but he definitely was not alone!

Jesus once said, "I will never leave you nor forsake you." And he was keeping his promise. What a beautiful way to go! Jesus also said,

> "There are many homes up there where my Father lives, and I am going to prepare them for your coming. When everything is ready, then I will come and get you, so that you can always be with me where I am." (John 14:23, TLB)

It is the promise of a home for the vagabond soul! "Let not your heart be troubled, you believe in God, believe also in Me." (John 14:1) Believing in Jesus is the full price of the home.

It doesn't matter what sort of people shaper you are, whether a genetic engineer or a wrestler, when it comes to the lonely act, we are all equally alone without Jesus. There is no other alternative!

"Our Father which art in heaven..."

15

The Saga of
The Little Bean!

A little bean is gently patted into the rich black earth. Soon comes a heavy dew and then a shower. The bean drinks in the moisture and soon a tiny sprout begins to shoot. One bright sunny day the little bean bursts through the earth to discover the sun as though such an experience had never happened before. But little beans have been bursting into the sunlight ever since the world began.

Once you believe in God, hear his footsteps and accept his love, the world and everything around you takes on a completely new look. The roses begin to show. The white-knuckle ride is over. You discover that a new life process has been going on for a long

time, generation after generation. Part of the new outlook is a dispelling of the gloom—not because the
world has moved off its collision course with disaster
—but because you realize that the most dramatic event
in the history of the human race could take place at
any moment. The world in general is about to be
caught completely flat-footed. The point is, there is
every indication God is about to blow his whistle.
There is very good reason to believe that we are the
last generation of little beans. It's like coming in near
the end of a show. A lot has happened before to bring
us to this very significant moment.

Old Mother Hubbard went to her cupboard only to
find it was bare. Mother Nature is approaching that
same dilemma. Her cupboard is slowly emptying.
Everyday things are disappearing off her shelf and
she is unable to put them back.

Our little space ship Earth, sailing so serenely
through a desert universe, is running out of gas—and
oil and water—and even food, especially now that the
third class passengers are insisting upon their share.
Actually with each passing day, the once-bounteous
little ship is looking more like an overcrowded life
raft with just enough supplies aboard to last for—well
that's the problem! For *how long?* And for how many?
And we might as well face it: how and when do we start
shoving whom overboard?

Mother Nature is letting us down! We have placed
more confidence in her than she deserved. For all our
adulation she has never been anything more than a
vending machine. All along we have overlooked someone very important. Our new insight tells us someone

packed us a lunch for a journey and that someone knew just how long the journey was going to be. We are coming to the end of it and we have on board all the groceries we will ever need. They will run out when the journey is over. However, nobody as yet seems ready to push the panic button. Instead people are devising elaborate schemes to limit the hands that can get into the lunch box. That way we can sort of eke things out forever, however long that may turn out to be. After all, what's the alternative? The only alternative to the empty cupboard is God. It may sound like a panic solution, but let's panic and turn to him!

Professor Killjoy's announcements from his ivory tower are getting more alarming every day. Think tanks, operating as early warning systems, seem to be specializing in bad news:

"A global picture of food scarcity is now emerging with disquieting implications for hungry people and for world political stability ... we have no safety margins left ... man, unless he changes his habits, is simply destroying the earth and himself."

"The catastrophe is not something that *may* happen, on the contrary, it is a mathematical certainty that it *will* happen."

"The prevailing escapism is of such dimensions that it is bordering on insanity ... If we continue, we are heading for inevitable disaster."

Time Magazine, February 2, 1970 published a chart that estimated the capability of the earth to sustain life would be reached by 2000 A.D.—that's *almost tomorrow!*

There once was a time when we could live in splendid isolation. We had only our own madmen to worry about. We could almost pick and choose our battles at will. That time is no more. We are forced to share in all the hazards of the world. *Their* madmen have also become *ours*. *Their* cry for food in the morning is heard in *our* living room the same evening. Hate has become extremely inflammable. It can flare up in Beirut and launch missiles almost simultaneously in the North Atlantic.

Fairfield Osborn in his book *Our Plundered Planet* writes:

> We human beings are rushing forward un-thinkingly through days of incredible accomplish-ments of glory and tragedy, our eyes seeking the stars —or fixed too often upon each other in hatred and conflict. We have forgotten the earth, forgotten it in the sense that we fail to regard it as the source of our life. . . .

Here is only another half-truth that is killing us. If we insist the earth is "the source of our life," God help us! Our problems are far deeper than more Corn-flakes. To allow the enveloping resource dilemma to glue our eyes to the earth is only to remain at the deceptive shrine of Mother Nature.

Mother Nature's story is a story of the common struggle to stay alive—with no one succeeding. Largely unnoticed, she is busy everywhere, destroying without mercy everything she creates. In the midst of her dazzling world of beauty she grimly operates her own house of horrors. From the lush green forest under-growth comes a little squeak of terror, then silence. An early morning song in the tree tops suddenly ends in a shuddering squawk. The proud and the fleet eventually stagger and fall. Such is nature's story: short mystical bursts of life, then death. Always there is the lifeless form, the broken heart, the empty, aching arms, the impenetrable wall we long to reach through. And frustration will remain as long as we look to nature as the source of life. Our dual dependency on Mother Nature and Human Nature is deadly. It is our undoing. Thus, we have come to a fracture point in history. We are not running out of *things,* we are running out of *time.* This could easily be the limiting factor to the normal life expectancy of any one of us.

We must not become totally overwhelmed by the threat of planetary exhaustion. It will not be decisive. Eternal life is the premium resource today, the bread of the future. In abundance now, it is the one resource that can vanish from the earth at any moment, without any further warning than we already have. Yet eternal life is the only answer for this dying planet. The source of our life is Jesus Christ. He said:

"My purpose is to give life in all its fullness." (John 10:10, TLB)

"In all its fullness" means the complete opposite to Rachel Carson's *Silent Spring.* It is entirely apart from earth life. It has nothing to do with the survival of seals or whales or the American eagle. It does not leak through your pores a day at a time. He said, "Because I live, you shall live also"—and he means forever!

Before Charles de Gaulle "passed on" he said, "The

91

world is undergoing a transformation to which no change that has yet occurred can be compared, either in scope or rapidity." No, the plot can't be passed off as an old re-run. What is happening now is strictly first run. Put all the pieces together and you'll see that nothing like it has ever happened before! Israel is back in its land, threatened for its very life by hostile powers on every side. Whether we like it or not the star of David is flying over the ancient city of Jerusalem. Europe, the USSR, and China are on the chessboard exactly where God said they would be at this time in history.

Some people get up tight that Israel is his point of historical reference. Suffice it to say it was his choice. He chose Israel as the sundial for what's to come. Israel is the key. Standing in the heart of Jerusalem, Jesus said that tiny nation was shortly to be dispersed all over the globe, but when its people were back in their land a series of related events would happen that would have special significance for the whole world. He went on to outline what this combination of events would be:

"When you see Jerusalem surrounded by armies," (Luke 21:20)

"When you hear of wars and rumors of wars," (Matthew 24:6)

"When you see famines and earthquakes in various places," (Matthew 24:7)

"When you see men's hearts failing with fear for the things that are taking place on the earth," (Luke 21:26)

"When the Good News is preached around the world," (Matthew 24:14)

"When the love of many (for God) grows cold," (Matthew 24:12)

"When you see these things know that I am at the door." (Luke 21:31)

"I am coming when you least expect . . . remember, I have forewarned you." (Matthew 24:44)

"These things will all happen during the span of one life time . . . and then you will see the Son of Man coming with great power and glory." (Mark 13:26, 30)

Professor Killjoy and all the Doomsday prophets of the mid '70s may eventually be charged with public mischief or disturbing the peace, but when we see this series of events coming into single focus, we surely are approaching the moment when clearly only two options are left. One is blessed, the other bizarre. We are back to the choice that confronted our first parents —God or Satan? The world today seems to be overwhelmed by a self-destructive urge, which introduces the greatest death-defying act in the history of the human race: receiving Christ into our lives before the whistle blows!

He is easily the most significant personality in the world today. The time has come for a serious look at One who is so much a part of our future. . . .

Good old Mother Nature!

16
The Incredible Journey

"It was like a giant Roman Candle exploding in the midnight sky and remaining suspended over the earth." His entry into our world invites such a metaphor. But it is not enough. It doesn't begin to tell the story. Most of the world's peoples count their days from the time he first appeared. But even this does not do justice to his person. Historians seeking the ultimate tribute have described him as:

"The time piece, the centerpiece of history;"

"The greatest impact for good on our planet;"

"The man whose life and death changed the course of human history."

We all find it hard to believe anyone could be deserving of such praise. But even when every word is true, the full story of Jesus is still not told. The Truth begins to dawn on us only when we wonder why each person who comes to know him falls before him in worship.

He has caused strange things to happen to human hearts. Galley slaves still chained to their oars suddenly felt free, exultantly free. Selfish, savage hearts unexpectedly were moved to tears at the misery of others around them. Serfs, held of less value than oxen, found themselves to be of human worth. Sadistic emperors bowed in shame as they heard the story of Jesus.

The name of Jesus is as vital today as ever. Every hour of every day some person is coming into dazzling new reality because of him. He *is* today; he *is* now! From where we stand he is more the future than the past. God's long arm of love knows no boundary of time or culture.

Only recently the famous warrior chief Tariri of the Shapra tribe deep in the far reaches of the Amazon jungles cried out, "God forgive me, I have killed, I have hunted heads." In the political center of the world, Washington D.C., Chuck Colson, a man described as tough, wily, nasty—The White House's hatchet man—bowed his head and prayed "Lord Jesus, I believe in you, I accept you, please come into my life." Just by speaking these words a wonderful assurance entered his soul. Old fears, tensions, and animosities drained away. A jungle chief and a presidential adviser, in different cultures and thousands of miles apart, were being "born again."

No wonder the question first asked of Jesus still requires an answer:

"What manner of man is this?"

Who then is he? What is he like? What is he *really* like? What can we know about him for sure? Centuries before he ever came, God told his prophet to write:

"and his name shall be called . . . the mighty God, the Everlasting Father, the Prince of Peace." (Isaiah 9:6)

The mighty God as Jesus came and lived in our own dimension exactly as foretold some 800 years before. *But why?*

Because God, before it all began, ordained that Jesus would declare his heart to everyone of us. He became our one chance, our last chance, to escape the coming darkness. But how would he be received?

For most of us his coming is an unwelcome invasion into our personal life. We reject him out of hand because he threatens so much that we enjoy. Again the same prophet who foretold his coming faithfully recorded the hostility that would meet him:

"But, oh, how few believe it! Who will listen? In our eyes there was no attractiveness at all, nothing to make us want him. We despised him and rejected him . . . We turned out backs on him and looked the other way when he went by . . . But he was wounded and bruised for *our* sins! . . . But who among the people of that day realized it was their sins that he was dying for? . . . His soul has been made an offering for our sin." (Isaiah 53, TLB)

The prophet described this generation before Christ

came and this is exactly the way it happened! His incredible journey ended on the cross! Or so his enemies intended. A truth too high for the mind, but easily within the understanding of the heart is his resurrection from the dead. God had come down from his high place of glory to our very doorstep. He let us drag him from that doorstep to the cross and to the tomb. For him, the resurrection was the easiest part of it all! The agony of his journey was the Cross. But that was where God's love and our downhill slide intersected.

Let's look at that intersection of divine love and human failure more closely. In the following chapter, mingle in spirit with the crowd as though you were there, witnessing the most appalling scene in human history.

17
The End of
The Beginning

The surging mob is strangely quiet as it crowds up the narrow street. Above the low din you hear an occasional shout, a hoof against the cobble, or the rattle of a wheel as it lurches over a hole in the road. The eerie silence seems to anticipate an awesome outrage. Some are drawn along, their mouths parched, ghoulishly fascinated at seeing a life about to be taken. Others in the crowd are fully occupied with their hate. But occasionally you hear a stifled sob.

In the midst of the crowd are the condemned. Three haggard, tired men. The two in front carry crossbeams over their shoulders. The third man walks behind, alone, his hands tied before him. His footsteps are labored and at times he almost staggers. He has been badly beaten and abused. His clothes are torn and stained with blood, and a crown of thorns has been crushed down awkwardly upon his forehead. Blood, now dry and hardened, mats his hair and stains his neck and face. This man is the object of the hate and fear—and from a few, the devotion—emanating from the crowd.

Despite four soldiers who walk around him, ruffians in their filthy tunics and wretches of the streets break through the guard to spit on him and strike him with sticks. Following close behind are a few men of high degree, conspicuous by the broad fringes on their garments and their fine cloaks. They discreetly feed the angry passion when it shows any signs of diminishing. Pushing and crowding, men struggle to look between and over the heads of others, to see the tragic, yet serene figure of the Nazarene. Surrounded by staring faces of unmasked brutality, the procession of the condemned moves slowly and painfully.

Finally they climb a hill. The slopes are dry and dusty, without any vegetation except for a few patches of scrubby hyssop. On the summit the procession stops. After a brief moment of turmoil, a universal hush descends. Then the sound of dull, hammering blows breaks into the silence and above the sea of staring faces, a cross appears stark against the sky. On it is the Nazarene, naked and scourged. His lips move and those on the hill and even far down the slopes hear him say, "Father forgive these people, for they don't know what they are doing." (Luke 23:34, TLB) Some standing at the foot of the cross know that a word from him, a breath, or even a thought can stop it all within a moment's time, and they painfully wonder why he lets the horrible scene continue.

Darkness unnaturally begins to creep over the earth. The air itself cools as daylight fades away. The two thieves beside him moan in their agony. Men look curiously at each other doubting what they see. From one of the crosses beside him a voice says, "Lord, remember me when you come into your kingdom." Surely the thief is wrong. To those watching he speaks only to the figure of a man helplessly impaled and broken. The pain of his dying must be affecting his mind. Still, the thief is so close. From his own cross he can see more clearly than those below. He can look right into Jesus' face. He can watch him breathe and hear him pray. He calls Jesus "Lord" as though a great truth has suddenly come upon him. The Nazarene, turning his head toward the thief, replies, "Today you will be with me in Paradise." Such strange words! What do they mean? Is this the key to why he has allowed himself to be siezed and so senselessly abused: so that the despairing wretch beside him can go free? Some that are watching and hearing shake their heads in remorse and return down the hill, wondering at the things they have just seen.

Those remaining now stand in total darkness. The ground beneath their feet first trembles and then begins to shake violently. Loose rocks are heard rolling down the hill, breaking themselves upon each other. Then, as quickly as it started, the earthquake is over and the frightened mob stands in the dust and silence. Suddenly everybody hears it—just three words spoken ever so clearly—*"It is finished."* (John 19:30) The words come from the center cross. The crowd shuffles in bewilderment. What does all this mean?

Traces of light slowly return to the sky. But somehow it seems like more than just light is appearing. Unexplainable as it may be, black clouds are lifting, chains are breaking, and some unknown cosmic battle has been won. A soldier looks up at the now lifeless body of the Nazarene and cries, "Surely this was the Son of God." (Mark 15:39)

His was indeed an incredible journey, from unmeasured glory into depths unknown. Now was the time for his return to glory. These are his words:

> "Father the time has come . . . I have told these men all about you . . . I have revealed you to them . . . and now Father, reveal my glory as I stand in your presence, the glory we shared before the world began." (John 17:1, 6, 26, 5, TLB)

Looking at our world you would never know it, but on that fateful day light won. Its bridgehead against darkness can never be threatened. But now the battleground has moved. The battle now rages in individual hearts.

Yet the victory *has* been won and the inner urge to self destruct can now be overcome. Each time the battle is won, the strange phenomenon of the hill of Calvary is repeated: clouds begin to lift, chains break, an unimaginable peace settles over the soul. This is the presence of the Nazarene. The cry of the centurion becomes our cry, "Surely this *is* the Son of God."

18
Why Did He Die?

It wouldn't be right. It wouldn't be fair to keep it a secret. It would be the meanest deception to even superficially scan his life and not consider as honestly as possible why it was that Jesus died.

A time is coming in the future that nobody wants to face. We block it from our minds, we stop our ears and we shut our eyes to keep every thought of it out of our lives. But still we know it must happen. It is the time when we reach the very end of the path!

Everybody knows that God must have a showdown with sin. Even those who have taunted "God, why don't you do something?" know in their secret hearts that a showdown has to come sooner or later. Justice, fairness, God's holiness—these make a showdown inevitable.

It has to be a holocaust! It has to be a thorough purging of all the evil that has scourged the earth. No trace of it can ever again be left to smolder and grow. God must deal with it once and for all, or he isn't God! The total malignancy must go! We know it, we sense it, but we cannot bring ourselves to face it. We dread it, we temper it, we reject it, but nevertheless at the very end of the garden path, there it is!

The prophet Daniel had a vision of this showdown and when he saw it he said, "I, Daniel, fainted and was sick many days." The apostle John had a similar vision and he saw

> "fire flash down from heaven and consume them, and Death and Hell were thrown into the Lake of Fire. And if anyone's name was not found recorded in the Book of Life he was thrown into the Lake of Fire." (Revelation 20:14, 15, TLB)

And Jesus said of that time that men will weep and wail and grind their teeth. The man who cannot lie said it!

> "For we are not fighting against people made of flesh and blood, but against persons without bodies ... huge numbers of wicked spirits in the spirit world." (Ephesians 6:12, TLB)

A head-on clash between God and the spiritual forces of evil is scheduled for the near future and there is no such thing as being caught in the middle! We will be caught on one side or the other. That's just the way it is! O God, have a heart—save us from such a day!

> " . . . and he was taken out of the city, carrying his cross to the place known as 'The Skull' . . . there they crucified him." (John 19:17, 18, TLB)
>
> "For God took the sinless Christ and poured into him our sins." (2 Corinthians 5:21, TLB)
>
> "He himself bore our sins in his own body on the tree, so that we might die to sin and live for righteousness." (1 Peter 2:24)
>
> "The blood of Jesus, God's Son, cleanses us of all sin." (1 John 1:7)
>
> "Since, therefore, we are now justified by his blood, much more shall we be saved by him from the wrath of God." (Romans 5:9)

Nobody needs a sermon to describe what took place. Even little children easily understand. When the final showdown comes, only by preference need any be present. Those who have been separated from their sin by the blood of Jesus will not be any part of it.

19
Quite Early
Some Morning

There is something inexpressibly delightful about a very early morning, watching and listening to the earth come awake. Everywhere bustling and stirring greets the new day. Little creatures curiously peek out from the covering where they slept. Wings swish overhead as birds begin again their search for food. From the undergrowth and from high in the trees, myriad little voices fill the air. The morning brims with new life, celebrating the rising of the sun.

The Sunday morning after the Crucifixion overflowed with new life too. The grave that had held Jesus for three days could hold him no more. As convincing as any historical event can be, his resurrection is.

Standing before many witnesses he said:

> "Why do you doubt that it is really I? Look at my
> hands! Look at my feet! You can see that it is I,
> myself! Touch me and make sure that I am not a
> ghost! For ghosts don't have bodies, as you see that
> I do!" (Luke 24:38, 39, TLB)

There is no need to persuade anyone that it happened. When the time comes, it is the most natural
thing in the world to believe. Life out of death is his
trademark! But it has no meaning at all until you receive the truth of it into your own soul. Then, brim-
ming with new life, you too can celebrate the rising
of the Son.

Just before the sun appears, a deeper darkness
seems to settle over the early morning. At that moment a star stands out in the sky more brightly than
any other. "I," said Jesus, "am the bright Morning
Star." (Revelation 22:16) Watch for him, for at that
very moment he will appear. The human family will
continue on its downward path into more lasting darkness, but for those who have been watching, quite
early some morning, he will appear. And he will take
them to a place where there is no night, no death, no
more tears. For them all these things will have passed
away.

20

"Prove Me Now"

So he died! So he rose again! So he is coming soon! So what? Who cares? It's a fair question to ask and sadly enough the answer is that not many do care. Millions upon millions do, but there are billions who don't. All their attention is given to maintaining an acceptable crisis level in their own lives. They do not see God as a helpful solution to their problems. The truth of Jesus' resurrection and its personal implication is of as much interest to them as continental drift or the migration habits of reindeer.

If you don't have a problem, you don't need God. But if you *do,* you *do!* Problems start with birth, and unfortunately they do not end with death. God has demonstrated beyond any reasonable doubt that whatever our problems may be, he wants to be the solution.

As we lay our problems before God and seek his help, it is vitally important that we see him as he really is. The center of his purpose, his very heart and nature, is to bless his people. Any other profile of God must be viewed from this light. No one in the whole universe is more on our side than God. More than a mother, more than a father, more than a husband or wife, God desires to share his love with each of us. He wants to see us so established in his presence that we can live above whatever our circumstances at any moment may be. He wants us to be able to wake up each morning and confidently say, "Good morning, Lord. What wonderful thing have you in store for me today?" and having said it, never look back.

When our greatest need is a friend, he says he wants to be our friend, even closer than a brother. When we are urgently in need of comfort, he promises, "I will not leave you comfortless." (John 14:18) And when we are almost smothered in our frustrations, he assures us he will "set us free." (John 8:36) Many times we are limp with anxiety and the big storm rages within, yet his promise holds true, "My peace I give unto you." (John 14:27)

We may continue to push the thought from our minds that sooner or later the fuse inside us must burn itself out. But putting it out of our minds does not put it out of our lives. First we face it in the lives of others, then we must face it in ourselves. For this ultimate problem, Jesus has the ultimate solution:

"I say emphatically that anyone who listens to my message and believes in God who has sent me has eternal life." (John 5:24, TLB)

Eternal life can be yours for the asking! The difference between a winner and a loser is *God!*

O God, have a heart! *God is all heart!* We say it in awe and wonder. His love overflows the whole earth. The mess of our world is only because of the world's indifference to his love. To be meaningful, his love must be personal. He so wants to wonderfully bless us, but he can only bless us as we will let him.

Regardless of which end of the crisis scale we are operating on—just the problem of being born, the problem of facing death, or any problem in between— a loving, caring, blessing God is saying:

"Prove me now! . . . and see if I will not open the windows of heaven and pour down for you an over- flowing blessing." (Malachi 3:10)

What an offer! And one we can't easily overlook! When the God of the universe says "Prove me now," the next move is clearly ours!

21
Long Live Me!

"Heads I win, tails you lose." It's a terrific game if you can find someone that will play it with you. Playing the regular game with a two sided coin you have one chance in two of winning. Half the time you can lose. With bad luck you can lose all the time. But if you ever do find someone that will play "heads I win, tails you lose" with you, don't miss the opportunity! It's the ideal house rule for winners. The odds against you are nil. *You always win*—and the one who is playing with you always loses!

When you come right down to the bottom line, the world has only two kinds of people: winners and losers. Vince Lombardi, once the great coach of the

Green Bay Packers, put it this way, "Winning isn't the only thing, it's everything."

The race however is not always won by the swift. The surest looking winner often turns out to be a loser. And it can so often happen that somebody on the bottom of the pile wins it all. At one time in my life I got so frustrated betting on horses, I started to bet on the jockeys. Neither system worked. A business associate who classified himself as "swift," gambled the lives of his whole family on starting his outboard motor just two hundred yards above the falls—and lost. The distance between winning and losing can often be your life. As Vince Lombardi said, *"Winning is Everything."*

In this chapter I want to tell you I have found somebody that will play "heads I win, tails you lose" with you. You can't enter into it lightly. If you really understand what you are doing it will move you to tears. The game was played first on the cross. Jesus deliberately played the game knowing he would lose because he knew it was the only way that you and I could ever win. Each of us must personally let the significance of this sink into our innermost beings until it draws from us a blending of sorrow, praise and worship. Only because he was willing to play the role of a loser did the Gospel for Winners come to be written.

"Who shall separate us from the love of Christ? Affliction? Or distress? Or persecution? Or famine? Or destitution? Or danger? . . ." (Romans 8:35)

"In all these things we are more than conquerors through him who loved us." (Romans 8:37)

"For I am convinced that nothing can ever separate us from his love. Death can't, and life can't. The angels won't, and all the powers of hell itself cannot keep God's love away. Our fears for today, our worries about tomorrow, or where we are—high above the sky, or in the deepest ocean—nothing will ever be able to separate us from the love of God demonstrated by our Lord Jesus Christ when he died for us." (Romans 8:38, 39, TLB)

"If God is on our side, who can ever be against us?" . . . (Romans 8:31, TLB)

"I can do all things through Christ who strengthens me." (Philippians 4:13)

"Who is he that overcomes the world but he that believes that Jesus is the Son of God?" (1 John 5:5)

The magnitude of these promises comes upon you as a rolling surf on a rising tide. Higher and higher like an endless ocean of waves the truth of it all keeps rolling in over you! How great and mighty is our God!

It was never more apparent than on that New Year's day at the Legion home. As the Good News was being read and songs of praise were being sung, you could hear an old man in a quiet sense of worship whispering, "Hallelujah! Hallelujah!" He had a twinkle in his eyes and light in his soul that just wouldn't go out. He had recognized the reading of the Gospel for Winners. He was a part of it and he knew it. That was the secret of Sidney Jeans!

Time and circumstance had not been able to defeat Sidney Jeans. He had too many things going for him. He was immovably in the center of God's love. For all his years, he knew he had barely started to live. It was only the beginning of the beginning. Before him was high adventure easily excelling anything out of the romantic history of the past.

"Hallelujah!" is the shout of winners. It is the ultimate expression of one whose heart is full of joy and praise for his Lord!

22
The Double Take

Just in case anyone doesn't know, a double take is a delayed reaction of surprise or dismay not initially captured by the emotions. It is aftershock surpassing even initial shock. It comes in two varieties—sheer delight and sheer disaster.

"Just letting life happen" is like pulling the clouds down closer around you and hoping somehow you will luck out! This comes under the variety of sheer disaster.

Need it be said the sheer delight variety begins with a personal relationship with Jesus Christ. He is the center of it all. His entire incredible journey was just to win for himself the right to stand at the door of our rebel hearts and wait to be invited in.

We have met in these few pages a variety of personalities, dear old Bill, dauntless Dan, positive Pam, Sidney Jeans, a little girl in leotards, and a host of others identified more by their thoughts and attitudes than as distinct personalities. The Lord loves each one of them. His patience and concern for them and each one of us is inexhaustible. The only limiting factor is the time that is ours to respond. When there is an urgency, there is no better time than "now."

There is a double take in your life! It will not happen by chance, only by choice. If you have never done so before, why not begin now a personal relationship with Jesus Christ. Invite him into your life and gratefully acknowledge his presence. Just say "Thank you, Lord, for forgiving my rebel heart, for dying for my sins, and setting me free." This is the starting point for a new life of blessing, joy and peace.

Having done this, the events of Calvary are repeated in your own heart—the clouds begin to lift, fears, pressure and doubts will disappear. For some it will happen instantly, for others more gradually, but the work of God's grace is done, the spirit of Jesus Christ dwells within you and you are forever on your way to heaven. All that is ahead for you is the aftershock of sheer delight. When you really think about it, it's the only way to go!

Bibliography

Anderson, U. S. *The Magic In Your Mind*. Hollywood: Wilshire Book Company.

Ardrey, Robert. *African Genesis*. New York: Bantam Books, 1977.

Britannica Yearbook of Science, 1970.

Gardner, Martin. *Relativity for The Millions*. New York: Macmillan, 1962.

Huxley, Aldous. *Brave New World Revisited*. New York: Harper and Row, 1965.

Jung, Dr. Carl. *Modern Man In Search of His Soul*. New York: Harcourt Brace Jovanovich, 1955.

Menninger, Karl. *Man Against Himself*. New York: Harcourt Brace Jovanovich, 1938.

Miller, Samuel, Paul Tournier, *et al. Are You Nobody?* Atlanta Georgia: John Knox Press, 1966.

Packard, Vance. *The People Shapers*. Boston: Little, Brown & Company, 1977.

Reid, James. *God, The Atom and The Universe*. Grand Rapids, Michigan: Zondervan, 1969.

Russell, Bertrand. *Autobiography*. New York: Simon & Schuster, 1969.

Wald, George. *Scientific American Magazine Editors. The Physics and Chemistry of Life*. New York: Simon & Schuster, 1956.